I dedicate this book to my loving Grandmother who always believed in me and taught me so many life lessons. To my husband and three beautiful children, thanks for allowing me to live out my dreams. To my mother, thank you for supporting me every step of the way. To God be the glory for the wonderful things he's done.

Thank you!

ISBN-10: 1541122526
ISBN-13: 9781541122529

GO AND GROW

By
Torri Hammond

TABLE OF CONTENTS

GO AND GROW

CHAPTER ONE

Fight

"In all your ways acknowledge him and he shall direct thy paths."
- Proverbs 3:6, KJV

My journey as an entrepreneur could not be without prayer. My life at the beginning of my Sasē Hair Care journey was long days, sleepless nights and hours of being on the Internet. It's hard to stay motivated when there is no money, or help in sight. Prayers for strength, and for provision, and knowing God was along with me for the journey is what gave me the willpower and the diligence to go on. I remember one of my demo videos reached almost a million views. You may be thinking, "Wow," but it was a wakeup call. People are rude, mean, and hateful. I love to communicate with people, so I wanted to read and respond to all the comments. I began to feel discouraged because of all the negative responses. Through my fight and prayer, I've reached deep to find out why I was so discouraged. I needed to understand that what God has for me is for me, and everyone doesn't have to purchase or agree with it, but as long as I fight first, everything will be just fine.

To this day, we have shipped to over thousands of people in a few different countries.

Call to Action

Before you can win as an entrepreneur, you must first learn to fight. You must always learn that you can do nothing in your own strength, or in your own abilities. When you set your feet to the plow, there will be storms and trials, but those who fight stand a better chance of persevering through to the end. Before you set your hands to do anything, fight.

F_{irst}

I_{n all things}

G_{ive}

H_{im}

T_{he glory}

Invite God along the journey and you will see Him do a work in you and your business, right before your eyes. Trust me when I say it's awesome to fight first.

Affirmation

I will depend on the greater He that is in me, than the He that is in the world.

Thoughts

_____

_____

_____

_____

_____

_____

_____

_____

_____

_____

_____

_____

_____

_____

_____

_____

_____

_____

CHAPTER TWO

911

"Be stubborn about your goals and flexible about your methods."

—Anonymous

I remember my first 911 situation. It was early on. I was in my first six months of selling products online. At this stage, I was purchasing envelopes from Sam's Club and we were writing addresses with Sharpies. Then the day came when we had over 100 orders to pack. OMG, it was a 911 situation for sure! I called in some friends and we got it done. The Post Office hated seeing us and we hated going. Something had to change and fast. I did some research and found a way to print labels online with postage included and started ordering envelopes from Amazon online. It was a crazy day, but we perfected the process through learning what worked and what didn't. Now, things are easy only takes one to two people to pack over 100 orders.

Call to Action

As a business owner, you have to be ready, because at any time things can change in a moment, in an instant and it's not always so easy to shake it. Trust me when I say, it happens. You have to be able to recognize when it's time to activate 911.

9 times out of ten

1 or more things need to change

1 day at a time.

You must be committed to finding out the what and the why of your current situation and make the necessary changes.

Affirmation

I will always be ready to adapt to change when it is necessary to allow productivity and functionality in my life and in my business.

Thoughts

_____
_____
_____
_____
_____
_____
_____
_____
_____
_____
_____
_____
_____
_____
_____
_____
_____
_____
_____
_____
_____
_____
_____
_____
_____
_____
_____
_____

CHAPTER THREE

Leave

"Act as if what you do makes a difference. It does."
-William James

The growing pains of turning my bad habits into good ones was tough. Watching TV and talking on the phone for hours about nothing had to stop. When I set my goal to start a product line, shopping was no longer an option. As my relationships began to change and my business began to increase, so did my priorities. I had a friend tell me she missed me, and yes, it was tough at times, but I'm easily distracted and I limited as many distractions out of my life as I could. Now, I don't care to watch TV much at all, and I limit all my phone calls. I post on social media just about every day with ease. So much in my life has changed, from me turning away just long enough to create new habits that could help me build a better business, along with ways that I could learn and grow.

Call to Action

Your biggest turn around may be wrapped in your ability to leave. As an entrepreneur, it's hard to stay focused. Friends and family members don't understand why you don't call or come around as much, but you know that whom much is given much is required.

Level-headed

Entrepreneurs

Always

Value

Elevation

Why? Because we know that once you reach a certain level, it's not time to wild out. We know how much work it takes to be in the race, and only focus and true commitment is going to keep you there.

Affirmation

I will make time for what is important and will strive to make better use of my time.

Thoughts

CHAPTER FOUR

Busy

"Being busy doesn't always mean real work. The object of all work is production or accomplishment and to either of these ends, there must be forethought, system, planning, intelligence, and honest purpose, as well as perspiration. Seeming to do is not doing."
-Thomas A. Edison

Starting for me was easy because that's the type of person I am. When I set my mind to do something, it gets done! As my business began to grow, I suddenly became the boss of everything. I was always busy, I was making money but I became so overwhelmed with my growth and with finally feeling free to do the things I couldn't do before, that my business became my downfall and I began to unravel at the seams. That's when I realized that I needed help. While I was doing well working in my business, if I wanted to survive, I needed to get out of it and work on growing it from the eyes of a CEO. Being in business means taking ownership and it was time to get out of the state of being busy.

Call to Action

As a business owner, it's very easy to get "BUSY". Trust me when I say I've been there. We as business owners begin by working in our businesses instead of on our businesses. Priorities turn into when I have time, and the self-accountability we once had gets lost, and before you know it, everything spirals out of order. Yes, it's very easy to get caught up in the rut, the rut of being the boss of everything and always having to be at this place and doing this thing. It's time to slow down and shift your business back into shape starting with you, and understanding that as a business owner, "BUSY" simply means...

Bogged down

Unorganized

Stagnant and

Yielding the look of success

Affirmation

I am organized and seeking the help I need in order to succeed. I will no longer be "BUSY" but I will strive to balance my life and my business from the outside looking in.

Thoughts

_____
_____
_____
_____
_____
_____
_____
_____
_____
_____
_____
_____
_____
_____
_____
_____
_____
_____
_____
_____
_____
_____
_____
_____
_____
_____
_____

CHAPTER FIVE

Do

"If you spend too much time thinking about a thing, you'll never get it done."
-Bruce Lee

I remember when I first decided that I wanted to start my own line of hair care products. I went over and over in my mind wondering if I could actually do this. I ran the idea across a few of my friends just to see what their reaction would be. I found myself in a state of DO, overthinking everything! I felt like I needed a sign that said go. But in reality, I just needed to start. I did the research and I ran over the numbers, and at that time, I realized this would take more money than I had.

So, I started to cut back and save, and once my end goal was in place, I was no longer in my own way. I was now on my way to reaching my goal. I started as small as I could with just four products, and I won't lie and say I knew it all when I started, but I will say this. I became the change I needed to see, I decided to Just B and simply go and grow!! We now have eight products and two years under our belt and I'm so glad I started!

Call to Action

If you have a desire to start a business or create a product, be careful not to reside in a state of "DO". It's so easy to delay your start because you think you need a sign or everything has to be perfect. Don't allow yourself permission to use excuses as they "DO" not explain anything about why you haven't started! Just get started, we need your talents and your services. So go, and don't reside in a state of I have to "DO", Just B and remember...

Do not

Over think

It's not about perfection, it's about projecting. I didn't know it all when I started but you learn as you Go and Grow.

Affirmation

I will take action despite my thoughts or doubts and I will press forward to do the work it takes for me to win!

Thoughts

_____
_____
_____
_____
_____
_____
_____
_____
_____
_____
_____
_____
_____
_____
_____
_____
_____
_____
_____
_____
_____
_____
_____
_____
_____
_____
_____
_____

CHAPTER SIX

Work

"I never dreamed about success. I worked for it."
-Estée Lauder

Back when I first started really focusing on building my brand, I had a lot of willpower, but not a lot of funds. For me, moving forward was the only option. With no formal training, I started everything I could. I built my very first website by myself. I learned how to market and grow my brand from books and late nights with Google. I learned very quickly that only the work that you do for yourself will show up for you. I trained myself to look at posting on social media as a daily task, and I talked and talked until I was comfortable with doing videos.

To this day, I still manage at least one of my websites. It's so rewarding when I get a call to speak or teach. Even opportunities that drop in my lap because of the work that I do for my brand.

Call to Action

Are you doing the work? Don't just say what you're going to do, put together a plan of action. Set your feet in motion. Write the vision and watch how things change as you do the work and focus on growth. It may be tough but nothing that has been worth it came without test and trials. Purpose a plan of action and continue to work.

Working while waiting on

Opportunities to show up

Realizing it's not easy but

Knowing all things are possible with God, faith, dedication and willingness

Affirmation

I will be steadfast, diligent and committed to doing the work.

Thoughts

CHAPTER SEVEN

Market

"The secret of your future is hitting your daily routine."
—Anonymous

I remember all the pain it took to grow my business. Knowing what you want to do is one thing but knowing how you're going to get it out to the masses is another. Sase Hair Care Products was my new baby and I was super excited about it. Quickly, I realized that if I wanted to be taken seriously, I needed to step it up and become a marketer. At first, it was a difficult task but once I decided to become the me I needed to see, I began to seek out books and programs that I could learn from. Every day, I strive to let people know and feel that Sase Hair Care Products existed. As I became clearer about my why and committed to my goals, results began to follow. Then came the next phase, attraction.

Opportunities began to show up and I quickly had to catch up to the growth that occurred in our first year. We sold over 5,000 jars of Sase's Sleek and Chic Texture Paste through marketing on Facebook.

Call to Action

I always tell entrepreneurs that people are only excited about what you are excited about. This is so true. Who cares if you don't? It's so easy in this race to be old news if you don't take the time to market. Sundays are a great day to market as it's the day before your work week starts and you can update and plan. It's your business, it's your life. Set up and be sure to checkup. Create content, read, plan, do the numbers, create specials, update your social media, the list goes on and on.

Make sure to

Always be

Ready with a yes

Keep

Everything up

To date

When people check on your social media, what will they find? I hope it's not old news. Market.

Affirmation

I will commit to doing something every day that helps me to build and market my business.

Thoughts

_____

_____

_____

_____

_____

_____

_____

_____

_____

_____

_____

_____

_____

_____

_____

_____

_____

_____

CHAPTER EIGHT

Truth

"True power comes from standing in your own truth and walking your own path."
-Elizabeth Gilbert

There came a time when I began to lose people from my life who I thought were there to help me. They had their own opinions and ideas about what I was doing in business. That period in my journey was very challenging because I valued their opinions. I'm a bit stubborn, which at times can be good and sometimes bad. However, it ultimately helped me to trust my own process.

I was once told that I was losing money by choosing to grow slowly. I was asked another time, "Who was I supposed to sell my products to?" Talk about negative. Both times, with total confidence, I stood in my truth and what God placed in my heart. From the very beginning, I learned that I am only losing when I give up, and the only way I won't reach the world is if I choose to be quiet and I am not doing any of the above.

Call to Action

You will find that as a business owner, there is always going to be someone who feels they have good advice or that their opinion matters, but it's important as an entrepreneur that you only give thought to the things that add to your life and your business. We tend to feel we need the advice of others and that's okay. Sometimes we do, but God gave the vision to you. Don't be easily persuaded. Stand in your truth and totally trust that you got this. You have got to build yourself and your confidence to the point where you know and can understand what's for you and what's not. Don't be so easily persuaded. Stand in your truth and trust the process.

Totally

Rely

Upon

Standing in your

Truth

Affirmation

If God said it, that settles it. Truth is, I got this. Truth is, yes I can. Truth is, all I need, I have. Truth is, I am well able. Truth is, I don't need permission.

Thoughts

_____

_____

_____

_____

_____

_____

_____

_____

_____

_____

_____

_____

_____

_____

_____

_____

CHAPTER NINE

Lose

"Do just what others say you can't do and you will never pay attention to their limitations again."
—Anonymous

I recall a time in my life where I always sought the approval of others. Not that I needed it, but I just wanted it. After a couple of years of me shrinking myself due to me listening to the opinions of others, I decided to lose myself. Now this took a lot of confidence-building within myself as I had to learn what to expect, and what to throw away, what to accept and what to throw away. Once I began to grow, I changed from seeking to telling, and that was no better as I began to hear what I should, shouldn't and couldn't do. I decided to stop looking to others for what I already knew in my heart, to take those words and prove them wrong. This helped me in more ways than I could ever imagine. Now the worst and the best thing you can say to me is what I can't do. My response, "Just watch me."

Walking in God's confidence and in faith to trust the process is how I overcame and learned to turn the negative into positive results.

Call to Action

It's easy for people to tell you what you can and cannot do, but as an entrepreneur, you have to grow a thick skin and not allow others to throw your course, but instead allow them to motivate you to your next level, so learn to lose.

Let

Others opinions

Self-

Elevate you

Affirmation

I will no longer seek from others approval of the assignment that has been placed within me.

Thoughts

_____
_____
_____
_____
_____
_____
_____
_____
_____
_____
_____
_____
_____
_____
_____
_____
_____
_____
_____
_____
_____
_____
_____
_____
_____
_____
_____
_____

CHAPTER TEN

Lost

*"Opportunities don't go away,
they go to other people."
-Rodrick Samuels.*

Before I started my product line, I sold t-shirts and hair extensions. I was working at a school learning to be an instructor. The owner was teaching at a major trade show, and offered me his booth to vend at the show. I paused in fear and he saw it and said, "What's the problem?" I had a million excuses.

Fast forward to about four months later. The Sasē Hair Care launch. I was again offered an opportunity to vend. Now this time, I signed up but didn't follow through. Yikes. So many times, I let those opportunities go to others because of fear. Once I reached my peak with Sasē Hair Care, I knew I needed to expand my reach.

Trade show. The faith was real, as I learned about cost and expenses, building a team, and transportation. As I put my faith to work, things started to fall in place. I had no excuses. We did the show. It was awesome. We had a blast, and then I paused to laugh at myself for waiting so long to do something that I could've done so long ago.

Call to Action

Don't sweat the enemy. He's under your feet. Why are you looking lost? Things like fear and procrastination always leave you lost. Now is the time. Just because you think you're not ready, just because you don't have enough money, just because you don't understand the greater he that is in you, you feel like you shouldn't do it. Right? Wrong. Now is the time to realize that in all things and in all actuality, you are lost.

Leaving

Opportunities, money

Sitting on the

Table

Affirmation

I will not walk in fear. I will take risks and face challenges with an open mind.

Thoughts

_____
_____
_____
_____
_____
_____
_____
_____
_____
_____
_____
_____
_____
_____
_____
_____
_____
_____
_____
_____
_____
_____
_____
_____
_____
_____
_____

ABOUT THE AUTHOR

Torri Hammond is the owner of BASHD and the CEO of Sase Hair Care Products. She started as an entrepreneur at the age of eighteen as an independent hair stylist and has since grown her brand to reach the masses. Her passion for people and her willingness to help others succeed is why she chose to embark on a journey of teaching others to succeed in business by sharing her personal journey. In addition to being a full- time entrepreneur, she is a wife, mother and devoted Christian.

www.torrihammond.com

42965201R00029

Made in the USA
Middletown, DE
19 April 2019